Sun

poems by

Benjamin Nash

Finishing Line Press
Georgetown, Kentucky

Sun

Copyright © 2023 by Benjamin Nash
ISBN 979-8-88838-212-7 First Edition
All rights reserved under International and Pan-American Copyright Conventions. No part of this book may be reproduced in any manner whatsoever without written permission from the publisher, except in the case of brief quotations embodied in critical articles and reviews.

Publisher: Leah Huete de Maines
Editor: Christen Kincaid
Cover Art: Benjamin Nash
Author Photo: Emily Nash
Cover Design: Elizabeth Maines McCleavy

Order online: www.finishinglinepress.com
also available on amazon.com

Author inquiries and mail orders:
Finishing Line Press
P. O. Box 1626
Georgetown, Kentucky 40324
U. S. A.

Table of Contents

Yellow Bells 1
The Cotton Pickers 2
At The Church School 3
Fear 4
Duty 5
The Motor 6
The Mobile Clinic 7
The Squeeze 8
A Winter Day 9
Panther 10
The Wig 11
At The Barbecue Place 12
Sun 13
Glue Sniffers 14
Warm 15
Murder At The Old House 16
Fossil 17
Rationing Electricity In Honduras 18
Undiminished 19
Scratch Off 20
Milk Dish 22
The Afterlife 23
Android 24
The Transfer 25
The Politics of Scarcity 26
Dutch Oven 27
Visit to Rome 29
As If In Solitary Confinement 30

Blue In The Night	31
Snap	32
An Honor	33
Yellow Jackets	34
Fourth Grade	35
Navigation	36
Silence	37
City Lights	38
Down There	39
Fight For The Water Hole	40
Easter Island	41
Social Worker	42
The Western	43
The Old Men	44
Splendor	45
Butterscotch Sun	46
Baritone	47
Door	48
Begonia	49
Testers	50
Library	52
A Big Thing	53
Drift	54
Coyote	55
Purple Lights	56
A Cross	57
Alien Denies Predestination	58
Blue Light Dancer	59
Coffee Can	60
When It Doesn't Rain	61

Blue	62
Light and Dark	63
Indian Blanket	64
Old Pictures	65
Coneflower	66
Ice Cream	67
Bus Driver	68
Glue	69
Afternoon Shower	70
Light Depressed	71
Pie	72
Bomb	73
Wardrobe	74
Last Day	75
Something Simple	76
A Hot Day	77
Orange Flame	78
Stray	79
City Sky	80
The Gas Station	81
Agaves	82
Candle	84
Spin	86
Gives	87
Today	88
The Long Drive	89
A Shooting	91

The Yellow Bells

The light is in
little yellow
flowers, in the
bells, and we
electrify,
city, in the
bumblebees,
as if tiny power
plants, ring
all the bells,
no other light
on this dark
day, only in
the bees, the
yellow flowers,
a few yellow
M&Ms in my
pocket, a few
car lights,
in our hope
that it doesn't
rain today.

The Cotton Pickers

Flies, dust, the
cotton pickers are
children and they
see white in the
sun, their faces,
everywhere, on
their bare feet,
the long stretch
of the bag, the
dog watching for
rattlesnakes, a
Gila monster, in
the salt of their
sweat, and in the
clouds. They see
water in the rain
that doesn't fall,
a mirage, in a
mason jar in the
shade, a cactus,
and in the cotton
that will pay for
their new shoes,
a new dress, the
rent, food, and
a chance for the
cotton pickers to
go back to school.

At The Church School

The air raid siren is danger,
red devils on the way, so loud
your ears bleed, the bombers
coming in, on a high pole at
the firehouse, so loud you feel
you are melting, minutes from
a nuclear blast, a test, and
I feel the wings of red demons,
like when I had dengue, turned
red, looked like a tomato, a red
Martian, the danger of evil in the
world, our ears ringing in class
as we return to our school work,
our imperfections, our lives, the
problems, the games we play.

The church bells are soft, safe,
sun on your face, the meek, a
boy, a girl, and some of us
will go out into the world and
make a difference, white angels
touch our faces, each of the little,
white houses around our school,
each person, and some of us will
learn how to love you, touch
your face, and not some kind of
white mind, nonviolent, talking
without moving the lips person,
but someone with a smile, a
kind word, often, not every day,
calm, peaceful, just like a bell.

Fear

Malaise,

when the smog clears the sky is the color of
mayonnaise and it is put on thick,

the color of an old, white commode
in a cold house.

Meteors, comets, UFOs and even the
gamma rays are in,

aliens with white lasers
and big eyes.

The pressure makes your ears pop
and it is hard to breathe,

and it is a piece of cut ivory and
the big, gray buildings
are dead.

There is fear.

Some winter
days are white darkness,

and you have to be the
light.

Duty

As if
a heavy
gold bar,

a bomb,

a small
metal box
with the
answer to
violence,

a fire
truck
blocking
all traffic,

a white
work truck,

as if
a baby,

a working
man carries
a turtle
to safety,

a man
with a
red face
as red as
the big
fire engine.

The Motor

When I hear the bad refrigerator motor
I think it is like a mine shaft elevator
bringing up the men with their headlights
on and the minerals they dug out, groaning,
carrying the water from the roots of the
cactus, up my veins to my heart and then
sending the blood out through the arteries
with the good stuff, out across on a yellow
cable car with the heavy load, and finally
making it to these red blooms on the cactus
before they fall off, the few years that there
is still a little gold, more like coal to keep
me alive in my body, hear the motor strain.

The Mobile Clinic

A raven is eating a big potato,
or is it a crow, pieces of Edgar
Allan Potatoe in his beak, in
the little drawing with pencil,

and it reminded me of a man,
Casanova, red hair, waiting
to see the doctor, telling me
that Edgar Allan Poe was his
favorite author, the white in
the green of the raw coconut,
with the guards on the walls,

guns, uniforms, in the prison,
trustees with wooden batons,
a place where the dictators
put their enemies, and I saw
a boy run barefoot, no shirt,
run by the murders, maras,
the macabre, men desperate,
and this other man says that he
has been in here for four years,
he stole a tire, no trial, in the
old, colonial prison, palm trees,

poverty, and the doctor will see
each man, looking in suitcases,
a smile, in white tennis shoes,

and you know that in the black
avocado is green, and then you
see the yellow, the light, a man
that killed his wife, gave me a
clean shave, cool, steady, with
a straight razor, a man that went
to prison and turned his life into
something different and better,

a man that preaches on Sunday,
and I thought about Poe again.

The Squeeze

An old man is
A cold lemon in a giant,
hot hand,

         in
a squeeze,

everything is
white except a big, blackened
sun,

and the air conditioner
is turned off to save
money, buy food,

medicine,

         in
a black oven,

as if in a dark Twilight Zone episode,
the sun moves in on him,
closer and
closer,

burnt

black.

A Winter Day

When you feel
like a piece
of cold silver
that they dug
out of a mine
and the heater
in the truck
doesn't work,

and you are not
going to spend
the money
on it to fix it,

you can't wait
for the sun to
come up on you,

and you want to
drive on and on
until you get
to Acapulco,
the blue ocean,
and swim in
the warm water
like Elvis did,

and you press
your face against
the window to
get the sun,
a lot like these
doves on the tips
of the trees in the
shade with no
leaves on them,

looking at the sun
on a winter day.

Panther

When your skin
turns white and
you feel sick,

there is silence,

a little yellow light,
something is not
right and you feel
like you are one
of those rubber
trees waiting
to be sliced open
and then bled out.

A baby cries and
the old woman
runs to the truck,

slams the door,

she is afraid,

she is ready to
go and she looks
for the old man,

it is almost night,

she thinks about
the calves and
there is fear,

the sun like a
cat's eye in the
black trees in
the bottomland,

the sun sinking
into the black dirt.

The Wig

Dignified, stately,
I was going to argue
that separation of
powers also meant
a division of labor,
specialization, but
it fell off, a horse
stepped on it, a man
spit tobacco on it,
it turned brown, a
cat was seen playing
with it and I decided
not to go, smell it
all day, deal with
the blue jay, Madison
and his jokes, or have
Franklin, the others
stare at it, whisper,
faction against me.

At The Barbecue Place

In the fizz,
in the foam,
as if dipped in oil,
as if swimming in the Gulf of Mexico,

a thick sauce to cut through,
a smoky brown,
brown pelican,
bubble up

Coke,
and
a sun potato salad,
a brown paper bag as

brown as the walls,
the photos,
the blue
marlin.

Sun

cactus,
a drop of blood,
cut,

red beads,

boy burns
his feet on the white rocks,

big white,

junipers,
jump,

limestone green pool,

big black,

boy plays
bear,

a little yellow,
blue corn,

sky.

Glue Sniffers

Under a bridge,
the color of the skin,
the color of the rio choluteca,
the glue sniffers,
their dreams,
drift,
dirty
river away.

Warm

is the red in
the sweet
gum leaves,
as if children
you can
hear them
in the wind,

is a calico
cat sleeping
on the floor in
yellow, in the
sunlight, in
a cold house,
as if we are
in a Van Gogh,

is an orange
plane in the
blue sky and
it reminds
me of boys
burning pine
on dark nights,
listening to
rock music,
and looking
up at the stars.

Murder At The Old House

How can you step
on sticky figs or have
the neighbors steal
them if they are gone,

how can your mother
lie to you and tell you
that you are eating
apple cake without pears,

how can you read
To Kill A Mockingbird
and learn about tolerance
without the magnolias,

       the white blooms,

and how can you imagine
a limestone, green pool
by the cypress tree
if it has been cut down.

Fossil

In this sky
white stars,

white soft
piano keys,

little thin
starfish in
lights in a
blue ocean,

in a stone
now white

Rationing Electricity in Honduras

The stars didn't fall from the sky.
An ogre
opened
his night mouth wide,
ate the stars whole,
swallowed
them
into
a big black
hole.

The stars didn't fall from the sky.
It's blackout,
no light,
but
the children burn bright,
little stars
that
dream,
scream when the lights
flicker back on.

Undiminished

Brisk, business like on the TV,
and the oven door is open, the
heat is intense, a day after a
massacre, in orbit, around the

moon, I thought of the angel
in the yellow light in the chapel,
Goliad, the men burned, buried,
and the dream whip, white for the

people killed yesterday, a small,
white church, man in black, the
dead dancing on a blue flame of
violence before they leave us.

I'm on my way to work, stopped
in traffic, shrill, sunless, the black
grackles in the parking lot are
in frenzy, fries, bread, exhaustive,

but then, undiminished, I saw
three, in green, wild parakeets,
rise out of a crape myrtle, a little
pink still in the tree, fly over me,

and I felt a little better, a man
cleaning windshields for a dollar,
a quarter at the stoplight, past
the sun, into space to tranquility.

Scratch Off

It is a cold,
orange sun in
the black trees,

wearing shorts
in the mountain
pass in summer
and walking
through snow,

driving in my
little, white
truck for the
first time,

David Bowie
on the radio,

and it was my
aunt with the
jammed up
fingers from
arthritis and
smoking the
cigarette with
her big smile,

the cat on the
sofa watching
soap operas
and shelling
some peas,

that took me
to the Czech
hall to play
a Bingo card,

and it is when
you win and it
makes you feel
good and you
buy another
at the grocery
store and you

think about the
bills you will
pay off and your
vacation to the
beach in Hawaii.

Milk Dish

With the swish
of a cat's tail around the milk
dish
we lap up our children
until we are full,
content.

The Afterlife

I would prefer to be painted
a deep,
dark blue to keep me cool
and be Picassoed
into
odd pieces lined in white,
so
that even if I lose one,
I can always
fit my face back together.
Then I will lie in repose
here
with a red squiggle
of a smile.

Android

Android
they will know what Freud
wanted to know
so
that can totalitarian
you with robotic
brain cells.

They will put microchips
into a crow
first,
later into you,
a few
and then many.

Android,
bionic
as you are,
if you complain about
freedom of conscience,
science,
they will say
lunatic.

The Transfer

The walls,
tall,
red,
they take them out dead,
electrocute them,
inject them,
reject
them
on death row.

The walls,
fall,
red,
they take them in dead,
process them,
inspect them,
accept
them
on death row.

The Politics of Scarcity

In a line,
one, two, three little ones in a line
follow their mother across
the road,
no cars,
a quiet day.

They are headed for the water,
the cold water,
silent
like
on a church day.

Out of the sky,
no sound,
swoops
down,

the red-shouldered hawk
grabs one of the
raccoons,

desperate,
dark

and it doesn't rain.

Dutch Oven

I saw a woman
shape a piece of
silver into a spoon
with a hammer.

I would like to
believe that I was
made this way.

Some days I'm big
like a tanker
moving through
the Panama Canal.

On other days I
am small like this
Dutch oven that goes
to the youngest child,

sits in the fire in the
early morning and
turns into something
as the sun comes up.

I don't always sound
right like this old
cow bell that I have,

but I also hold a lot
of treasures like the
coffee cans used to
pick blackberries,

hold buttons, nails,
earthworms, black
and white photos,
or baseball cards.

I will wear out like
my old, red truck.

And then one day
in India they will
cut my old metal
into big pieces,

and there will be
a red glow and
I will start over.

Visit to Rome

Venus de Milo
can't ride a
Vespa around
Rome, comb
her hair, smoke
a cigarette,
or eat a piece
of cheese with
no hands and
arms, and her
mouth will
water, with the
spaghetti sitting
on the plate
uneaten, no
fingers to lick,
no hand to
apply the red
lipstick.

As If In Solitary Confinement

As if in solitary confinement,
as if Steve McQueen on Devil's Island,
she squints in the sun,
steps out

as if on cold tin,
as if in cold light.

She complained and complained.
I told her to take her problem to the
United Nations,
not listening.

As if a dissident,
as if in Solzhenitsyn's Soviet gulag,
she squints in the sun,
steps out

as if in cold water,
as if in cold light,

long suffering
indoor cat.

Blue In The Night

There is still blue
in the night by the
river, stars, closing,
the college, my job,
in my car I can see
deer, lightning bugs
on the golf course,
at the edge of the
dangerous part of
town, burglar bars,
a women's shelter,
buses, the library,
where last week a
man tried to grab,
kidnap a woman,
and when I get
home a polar bear
is in the blue ocean,
the white on the
edge of the blue in
the night over my
apartment, and it's
a TV dinner, steak
and tater tots on
a big, blue plate.

Snap

A pull,
then a rubber band snap,

black cat firecracker,
burning pine
snap,

it's not a tap,
it's the snap, snap, snap
of the ice tree gunfire,
green bean,
finger
snap.

Whip.
wet towel,
we need our snap,

it's in the night,
it's in the red hot brain,
blood
snap.

Bug,
big Einstein idea,
it's electric shock
adrenaline,

girdle
tight

snap.

An Honor

It is not Vera Cruz
or Okinawa.

In dock
old dreadnought,
and it is the thought
         that counts

for this boy scout
locking his
knees

on the deck
   of the Battleship Texas,
holding the American flag,
hot sun on his neck

as he starts to
go down.

Yellow Jackets

Face,
tractor is
        red,
     rage.

               Swarm
         is yellow,
sun bursts in the blood,
      a fever.

Fourth Grade

Big hair,
a blonde,
a bouffant,
Ms Pillack is on stage,
playing the accordion.

It's Agua Dulce,
a polka,

singing,
swinging her hips,
wearing horn rimmed glasses,

she is tapping her feet
intently,

a treat,
a teacher,

but no cowboy hat.

Navigation

Quick
the bats come out from under
the bridge,
fly

blind,
whispers in the
night,

impulses,
love swerving
unrequited

in and out among gargoyles,
quirks.

Silence

I can imagine,
barely perceptively hear

the tingling
at
the tips
of my fingers,
a light
tingling
after a sudden flash of lightning

a load drop,
accelerate
to
the
bottom of my feet,
slam
down,
as cars screech loud,
crash
into a stop

the elevator,
elate,
lift
in me to the top floor,
letting off
little passengers of happiness
when
rockets rise,
kiss
the sky

where there is silence,
just a second,
a sigh.

City Lights

In dark,
in dark pencil,
in dark dreary portable,
in dark dreamy city lights

a boy is drawing a city in an eye,

lined in tall skyscrapers,
a little slice of moon,
dangling as if
a lemon.

Down There

I didn't see the night watchman with his shotgun.
All the lights were out. There was fear in the taxi
driver's voice. He asked us if we lived down there.
He said that he didn't drive down there at night.
On the edge we got out of the car. The road in
the moonlight was like a cold coroner's table. We
didn't go down there at night either. I could see
down there from a high window in our apartment.
On most nights the lights were like one of those
white Christmas light strings, but not tonight. The
only lights in these blackouts were red. Ambulance
lights sliced through the night like cutting open a
fish and seeing the red inside. There were gunshots,
sirens, and the next day black and white photos of
dead bodies in the newspapers. When the sun rose
up, then, now, there will be men, women in the plaza,
a few children, the white cathedral, the palm trees,
the long row of shoeshines, lottery tickets, men with
folders standing outside the government offices,
talking, working, a police officer, and no one looks
at the photos, asks what happened down there, goes
there, the same thing every day, or helps the poor,
not today, tomorrow either, and they don't want to
see the blood, the sadness, the fear, their own fear,
and they won't ask any questions, look for the guilty.
The only thing they will do is pray, go to church on
Sunday, go to funerals, try to do the best they can.

Fight For The Water Hole

The Indians circle,
heads spin, closer
and closer, the sun
moves in, a man's
thoughts move in,
and with each drink,
shot, breath, bite,
drop of sweat, each
second the circle
tightens. On the
perimeter they are
pushing in, they
salivate, lick lips,
look in, wait, this is
a siege, and every
man rides fast
around, over and
over until their
horses collapse or
they die on the edge
of concentrated fire.

(my favorite Remington)

Easter Island

It's persecution,
no one talks, all of
them are in on it.
I can't see their faces,
feet, or what they
do with their hands.
I was pushed, fell over,
and now I can't see what
they do with their mouths.
I can't hear them, but
I know they are
all scheming, planning,
a mind-control project,
to see if they can
use silence to get
me to conform,
lose my spirit,
a rationalized man,
rules, norms, and
big institutions.

Social Worker

At 23 years old she must
seem like Tinker Bell to
these old people,

when she was four
she had a little
blue gown with
the yellow fairy on it,

I remember when
she caught the fire
flies and watched them
glow green in a jar,

day after day she
brings her smile with
her to sign them
up for cooked meals,

sometimes they die,

when she was born they
put her in an oxygen
tank as if she was
sent to us from space,

a little light in it,

wearing her
be good always
tattoo on her arm,

and she calls
us to help her
because she locked
her keys in the car again.

The Western

On the oil rig, at the
colonoscopy, sitting on
a white horse, a broken
toilet, in the divorce
lawyer's office, in the
fishing boat, on orange
chairs with your wife's
family, a man needs a
western, and a subway,
at the Laundromat where
no one speaks English,
the porch, in the ruins
of Copan, a hearse, on
the stand watching the
redheaded woodpecker,
the church service, the
long documentary about
Gandhi refusing to eat
a sandwich, the beach,
at the piazza, the café
with a plate of snails
and frogs, a man needs
one worn out paperback
about cowboys to read.

The Old Men

The blue heron in the dark pond,
tall pines, reminds me of the old
men, walking carefully, wearing
the beat up cowboy hat, a good
one for Sundays, getting up at
light to watch the beef prices,
going to bed when the sun goes
down, chewing tobacco, spitting
it into a coffee can, feeding the
cows in winter, cutting up the
pine, burning it down, growing
corn, tomatoes, beans, keeping
the rifle near the bed, knowing
how bad it was to use it, and
lifting, the blue heron, leaving,
slowly, men that worked on oil
rigs, cut lumber, grew cotton,
raised cattle, went to the city,
offices, the port, went to war,
men that were hard on their
kids, their wives, suffered in
the depression, were all about
values, men that saw us go to
space, saw Kennedy fall, and
now they are all gone, like the
cigarette, the smoke, is fading,
and the dark pond is now empty.

Splendor

You have a touch of pink
eye
this morning,
light in the sky.

Put in your eye drops,
at first bleary,
clearing
blue.

Don't blink,
ink
in your colors,
open wide.

All day,
stay
with us,
don't close your eyes.

Butterscotch Sun

Silent until
jack rabbit jump at twilight,
a self-reliant ranger
listening,

an armadillo,
soldiers from Mexico,
it's bitter cold sitting on this
deer stand,

dogs
chasing coons,
a yellow one if Texas,
cowboys roping wild cougars,

mesquite,
mean gunslingers
riding through the blackjack,
dark are their faces,

and there are steps,
sounds in the rustling trees,
around the
cactus,

whitetail,
maybe it's Comanche,
a boy heavy with reading
holds a rifle,

looking,
waiting,
warmed by a butterscotch
sun.

Baritone

There is a bull with a
ring in its nose
in my baritone,

a whooping crane,

a barking dog,

a black case,

it is heavy and it
is a long walk
to the bus stop.

I can hear the owl,

a freight train on
the horn and the
cars hitting together.

I can also hear the
morning sounds of
the newspaper
hitting the front door,
my father creaking
open the oven door
to put in the biscuits,
my mother gargling,
and the garbage
cans slammed down,

a boy,

a bear,

a tug and a foghorn in a
dented baritone and
here comes the bus
bright as a yellow light
bulb next to the gas station.

Door

Hummingbird, hammering on the glass
in the dark garage, each heart beat hard
to do now, each beat a heave, like the
old industrial fan my grandmother had
in the backroom, each blade turn an effort,
working the hot air out, sewing yellow
stars, sunbursts, and I open the door, hoping,
hurry, there is not much time, you need to
leave now, find the sun like the one in that
old quilt, more and more heavy you are,
and I think this might be what it is like
in the hospital, about to die, I'm yelling help,
and my grandmother, someone opens the door for me.

Begonia

This yellow begonia is blooming.
A woman was playing a guitar
and asking for money in traffic.
At the store a man wanted some
change to buy a bus ticket. It
was hot outside. On the news
I saw that another man returned
the music instruments that he
stole. He had taken them to his
tent underneath the overpass.
I flicked off the browns and
the dead from the begonia. He
probably gave the guitar to her
to make her happy. Maybe I am
wrong, but she didn't have the
guitar last week at this busy
intersection. The yellow is
about living, the joy that we
sometimes find and share.
I hope no one says anything
about the guitar. I pulled out
the bananas, the plantains,
the avocados, and the oranges
from the grocery bag to put
them away. A rock star died
today. He played the bass guitar
in ZZ Top. Each of us falls off
the begonia at some point in
time with our little lights. I am
getting older. My rock heroes
are dying. It was a long time
ago when we used to watch
all those videos on MTV all
the time. I watered the yellow begonia.

Testers

Babe Ruth once hit a home run over
the fence in Sing Sing prison
in an exhibition game, the men
excited, the ball ignited, up
in the air, on a white streak,

I imagine these men are like
that baseball in a way, to rise,
to make it over, a table,
a pencil, and a test booklet
for these men waiting in line,

the bars, the uniforms white,

it doesn't matter what they
have done, not on this test,

I read the instructions slowly,
they begin, silence except
for the clock ticking, all of us
nervous, a cough, a chair
scrapes the floor, lead breaks,
the test booklet is thick, they
fight it, glass, guard looks in,
the light in the window, white
at first, turns yellow when the
sun comes up, the testers tire,
thinking is hard, tough men,
tattoos, they finish, and leave,

sometimes a smile, but most
have on their game faces,
no expression, we stack tests,

men sit on white benches in
the hall near the infirmary,
wait, door opens, exit, driver's
license returned, and then
we break through, our car, guard,
a cowboy hat, pistol, barbed
wire, the gate, cows, on a farm road.

Library

I like how the big yellow locomotive
with the long line of cars passes
next to the library and blows its
horn loudly to warn the cars ahead.

I like how I can check out a video
of *The Treasure of the Sierra Madre*
to see Humphrey Bogart and others
fight for gold in Mexico in the 1920s.

I like how the boy rings the bell
that was rang to tell everyone that
WWI had ended years ago and
I like how his little sister rings it too.

I like how I can look for a children's
book, use a computer, and take a
discard book when I don't have much
money and I can use a little equality.

I like how there is silence and I
can look out the wide windows
next to the newspapers to see
the oaks outside and the American flag.

A Big Thing

A big thing is a little town where a Texas Ranger
couldn't prevent a mob from burning down
a courthouse, the black man accused
of rape inside, dragging his dead body
out to show these small children in the
crowd how to use terrorism for control,
his soul already gone, when people
don't know about nonviolence,
hanging, burning him over a bonfire.

A big thing is an old man today finding a
black man lynched in black ink on a
restroom stall door, when we have
made progress, when the intent is to
incite, to use violence to get your way,
to not work out our differences,
and this man can't wait for the police,
the janitor, he worries about these
students in this school, hurries to wash it off with soap.

Drift

A fog moving out or smoke drifting down the street,

a white egret flying low
or chalk dust,

it is none of these things,

it is concrete dust coming from men ripping
out the sidewalk,

I'm watching an old movie about
a woman in New York City
spreading smallpox and the authorities are
looking for her to quarantine her to
stop her from killing people,

when doctors and nurses wore white,

the men are taking a break and sitting in the
shade and the way the dust seems to float down past
us reminds me how easily people
are dying from the virus and fading away,

they get up to pour the new concrete,

have you ever seen a piece of
white paper or a balloon
carried off by the wind and then
watched it until you can't see it anymore,

it is a lot like that to me these days how people are leaving.

Coyote

Was it the sandhill crane or
the laughing gull in the glass
case next to our coyote,

was it the chemistry class
or the ostrich around the
corner that got him going,

maybe he wanted to sing
with a cowboy, cry like
a baby, be an Indian war
party, or an Italian opera,

maybe he wanted to find a
saguaro, a big stage, a mesa,
do Shakespeare, do Macbeth,

maybe he wanted to act
like Lassie, a tractor, a
man pinned down under it,

maybe he heard the wild
appaloosa horses, wanted
to see them, or longhorn
cows stampeding in lightning,

I couldn't figure it out,

maybe he heard drug dealers
shoot it out, a police car
with sirens on, a woman
screaming, an abduction,

maybe he could help,

outside was the coyote
headed out into the night
and I wanted to go back
upstairs to see if I was seeing
things at the community college.

Purple Lights

Raw, in my mouth, outside, wind, rain, gray,
my black umbrella, wet, it is coming down,
our water is going to be turned off, a break
in the line, with no hot water, old boiler,
and then in my truck in traffic, but what's
this, little pieces of purple on the gray hood
of my truck, as if little grapes, pieces of
happiness, parked under the laurel tree,
and in my bag a book about rattle snakes,
story of a cat protecting her kittens from
one, and isn't there always something to
look forward to, a Johnny Cash song on
the radio, engine, lights, the sun is coming up.

A Cross

An orange sun,

a white star,

the woman
has on a purple
dress and is
smiling in her
bare feet,

she has a big
red heart
for all of us
that need her,

a brown face,

and we thank
her for looking
out for us
in the cold
when we lost
our power
and the water,

letting the
dead marigold
come back
to us and the
hope in
the little leaves
of the blue
hydrangea
that survived,

on a wooden
cross an
angel with
her white wings.

Alien Denies Predestination

We have lost all power, the spaceship
is dead, we are like seamen in a
little yellow dingy in the ocean and
there is no one around, we are
waiting for someone to come along,
the stars are cold, lifeless here, as if
on a string being held in front of us,
the moon near us like a disco ball,
spinning around us, as if the gods
are putting on a show for us to see.

Your blue planet means dissection,
sharp metal tools, we might kill you
like smallpox killed the people,
the Aztecs, we are not sure that we
want you to find us, but we would
like to tell you about dead planets,
what they did there, that you will
never understand what good is
until you see what bad is, that you
believe in it, that you have choice,
that you can learn, we would like
to reach an island like you have
with tall coconut trees that might
fall on your head, stars come alive
in red, blue, that a submarine will
appear, yellow, and that we will
not die, be afraid of what comes
next when they take our bodies
out of this dead spaceship in our
yellow spacesuits and take us away.

Blue Light Dancer

The black snake was the car parking
next to our house with two
men getting out and
walking to our front door
lead by the red light dancer.

The Black-eyed Susan was the
effect of the lamp in my room
when I turned it on after
watching the blue light dancer
convince the men to go back
to their car and leave without
the lights on silently down the
street by the lawns that I
would later cut when I was older.

The bug-eyed white egg with the
yellow inside was the little
boy that I used to be that didn't
get eaten and I could not
hear the pluck, pluck on
the cello anymore that scared
me with the deep base since
it was returned to its black case.

The blue light dancer came
to tell me in her sad voice
that it was good that no one
got hurt and I was happy
that I did not have to get
my father sleeping in his bed
next to the garage to confront
the black snake because of the
bad things that might have happened.

Coffee Can

Buttons, blue, white, yellow, and picking berries,

black and white photos, thread, thimble, needles,

red coffee cans everywhere, nails, red and rusty,
they put everything into the cans, bolts, washers,

when a red wasp stung me on the ear, she broke
off a piece of aloe sitting in a can and squeezed
out the juice, tomatoes, pecans, and purple hulls,

he sat on the porch and spat red wads of tobacco
into the cans, silver, metallic inside, old railroad
spikes from the tracks that they took up, hammer,
pliers, bullets, black dirt, earthworms for fishing,

beans, red, bags from Colombia, El Salvador, all
the way to this faded little house, tin roof, sugar
cookies, cow medicine, notes, bills, gloves, the
barb wire cutters, red flowers in front, in and out,
screen door, orange candies, garden in back, tall
corn, watermelon, pencils, fabric, matches, bits,
pieces, each of them, look in the red coffee cans.

When It Doesn't Rain

Blue helicopter,
little thing
in a blue bucket when it doesn't rain,
it is hot and this is the
only water around,

tiny blue soldiers jumping out
are on a mission,
a blue sky,
it's raining
yellow leaves,

a dragonfly,
vibrating blue,
lifting,
the old people are filling apple juice and cooking oil
bottles with water,

as blue as my mother's blue hydrangea,
leaving,
I'm feeling a lot better,
water on the beans,
the yellow squash in the garden.

Blue

We waited outside the grocery
store in a line like they used
to do for toilet paper in the
old Soviet Union or in Cuba,

I saw a blue canoe tied on to
the top of a car in the parking
lot and I thought it would be
nice to float down the river
in silence without any fear,

a hundred years ago they
could still hear them hammer
the nails into their pine boxes
with their blue bodies still
a little alive with dying,

I saw the graves lined up in
a row in the rural cemetery,

it makes you sad and I know
my father is hiding in his
house and I am right on the
edge of old age myself now,

they die alone in a hospital
without a hug or a last kiss,

the virus brings suffering
and sorrow and you begin to
understand what the soul is,

at least the bluebonnet won't
make you sick if it touches
your face and neither will the
sun or the sky up above you,

nor will the people you know
waiting for you and your
blue face holding them at last.

Light and Dark

In the day I am a black window in a white
house with the lights all turned off
and at night I am a white window
in a black house with the lights on,

black, white, what might appear in
a noir movie, an old photo, with a
black, white cat, the yellows, reds,
blues inside me that you can't see,

I have never been a white window
in a white house with the lights on
or a black window in a black house
with the lights turned off in the day or in the night.

Indian Blanket

Yellow tips around the red inside,

as if nerves and in the blood,

I think of electricity flow, the
light, and about other things,

a yellow car with hot engine,

the sun is cool in the morning
when it touches your face and
far away from where it burns,

if you pull one flower from the
big field will it hurt all of them,

will they start thinking about it,

will they remember the buffalo,

will they remember the people
that were here a long time ago,

will they remember wild cows
and cowboys riding with rope
after them through the brush,

a yellow locomotive pushing
with a heavy load of red cars
full of oil, chemicals, lumber,
trucks, coal, beef, and grain,

girl with a pretty, yellow dress on.

Old Pictures

The yellow fever, a cradle,
on horses, in overalls,
a sick bed, soldier,
in wagons, hats on,
aprons, settlers, Indians,
and slaves, working cattle,
suffer, people don't have
anything to smile about,

poor, factories, no heat,
meat packing, break
your back, lose your job,
banks taking your place,

these dead bank robbers,
full of holes, lying
on pieces of wood,
aren't smiling either,

a man hanging, rope,
get blown up in a
railroad tunnel, mine
coming down on you,
one arm, one leg, don't
ever smile in a photo,

smiles are for your wife,
a new baby, a sunflower,
saving a white face calf,
the end of a long war,
smiles are not to be wasted,

thinking that this will end,
that you will see your
dead parents, things will
work right, you can forgive,
relax, some of these people
will go to hell, then maybe
you can smile just a little bit.

Coneflower

I saw the blue passion flower with two bees on it, but it was the Ruby Star coneflower
that I bought at the nursery with one bee that followed me
out to my truck, the petals sticking out, pink, purple, pretty, planted in the pot
with the orange coneflower, its petals bending down, unable to
spin like I imagine a flying saucer would, orange, pink lights in the night.

I thought about the fireman that they brought in on the red fire engine, the men in yellow and black coats, buzzing around outside, bees stinging their friend, dying inside, the sadness on their faces, a husband, a father not coming home in a poor country. I hope that someone gave him their hand when he got to where he was going, that he will get the promises that Robert Penn Warren talked about, that I heard about in church, that he won't be angry with the bees for what they did, accept what they do for us, and I would like to have seen an orange sun the color of the flower with a little blue in the sky, yellow and white flying saucers like coneflowers up above me, something special in them, that someone could tell me for sure that the fireman is happy.

Ice Cream

It was a bus stop and it was hot,

where the blue city buses stop,

it was so hot that everything
looked white outside to me,

close to where the moms
wait with their kids each
morning for the school bus,

I am in my apartment as if
each person outside is a
tiny leper colony and each
an enemy that I need to avoid,

it is the time of the virus and
I am thinking about a man
that I saw a few summers
ago asleep at the bus stop,

he was wearing a cowboy hat
and he was an old man that
looked like he was worn out,

beside him was a small white
ice cream cart that he had
been pushing hard all day,

it didn't seem right to me that
he had to push that cart and
it doesn't seem right that all
these people are dying now,

don't forget that each us are
little white cathedrals that
are special and unique inside,

good tasting ice cream that
sometimes melts and drips to
be sticking messes on the ground.

Bus Driver

bus
empty,

        the light inside the bus is a little bluish and
        in the building the driver sits on a bench in a blue uniform,

        ghosts gather
        around a tired man in the night,

        as if he is a porch light
        and they are bugs,

        as if he is the last
        angel,

        alone,

slowly
getting
up to return to his bus

Glue

White glue all over the floor,
on my feet,
on my fingers,

on the little tuxedo cat,
her gloves,
her shoes white
as the glue,

the kind of white glue
that holds the
little white
stars on a string,

coming up out
of the floor
as if it will
be a white blob that will
grow and grow until
it eats us,

enough glue to patch
up the sad,
the badly hurt
in the hospital,

in my head,
in my blood,

all over my tennis shoes,

the kind kids use to
stick red smiles
on white paper plate faces,

enough to stick
the sun
back up if we need to one day.

Afternoon Shower

It was a shower and gone
quickly. The sky was
only gray a short time.
It reminded me of a gray
fox that I spotted in the
city when I went to buy
two pizza slices, the
unseen people that pass
by us, ghosts that we
think that we see out of
the corner of our eye,
lightning that we are
not sure if we saw or not,
or a rat late at night on
a lonely street bolting to
the drain opening. It
may be me one day if I
decide not to go on.
I will be like this strange
old yellow Winnebago
that I often see in parking
lots, streets, trying to
make it in a difficult time,
moving always, caught
between the good, the
bad, looking for a home,
the sunshine, unsure
about where I am going,
looking for a better
place than what we have
here, the rain as light
as a cat running silently by me.

Light Depressed

It's hard to see the squat white
building, lights on inside are
slices of warm yellow
cake, rain, cold, like liquid
soap, like the sugar cane syrup
my grandfather put on his
biscuits, thick, cleaning the
concrete from oil, sticky, red
stuff, and once in I try to last,
I get light depressed in winter,
the weak light is like a dirty,
white softball all day, I burn
the daylight I stored up in the
summer and a few good days
in fall, hoping I do not become
a dead satellite, no power in
the solar panels, in orbit, held
down by gravity, with no light,
like my family's old black
lantern that they used before
they strung up the power lines,
the gray rain falling all day,
if only a big, yellow bulldozer
would push aside all of this,
it feels like one continuous
wash in a white machine in
the laundry, around and
around, I think I need to build
a white chapel like Sidney
Poitier did for the nuns in the
desert with the cactus all
around to distract myself,
find something to do until
sunset, until night, sleep, and
morning, a dryer, put in the
quarters, charge up like a cell
phone, start over, hope I smell
a fresh lemon, see it up in a
wide, blue sky, be positive about it.

Pie

Chocolate meringue pie is a white lily sitting on a dark pond. It is sweet tea after cutting the grass. It is the brown water at the beach in Galveston, the white foam, the seagulls, the oil tankers coming into the port red and blue. It is the magnolia, the jasmine, the azaleas, the rich soil, and about being better than in the past. I would like to go to a country and see them cut open a cacao with a machete, find a Spanish fort, and a palm tree. In the cafeteria, the cemetery, after church it is always fried chicken, fried okra, macaroni and cheese, a roll, and a piece of pie. I like to eat it cold sitting on a long porch.

Lemon meringue pie is a daisy with yellow inside it. I think it is light, a good person, a sunset, a hard day of work, and a cold room with a window unit air conditioner. I wonder about those desperate men that crossed the ocean with a few lemons for scurvy, the mercantilism, the natives, and what they did there. It is the sunflowers with a yellow locomotive pulling a long line of cars passing by them, the white clouds, the sun above. It is about lift. It would be nice to see lemon trees in Sicily, the Roman ruins, and the blue water. It is about visiting, playing cards, fireworks, fried catfish, and pie.

Bomb

He told us that he was working on that day
and how hard it was to talk
to the families because they couldn't
tell them yet about the bomb explosion
until they had more information.

I saw the pain in his face.

He was giving us instructions about what to do
if we got a call about a terrorist attack.

I wasn't good at selling airlines tickets and I didn't
work at that job very long. I always put the wrong meal
in the wrong place on the computer. I remember
one of the women looked like the lead singer of the band Blondie.
The conversation about Flight 103 was what
I took away with me. A new Pan Am was trying to start up.

I was thinking today about what kind of flight went to Lockerbie
to pick up the dead passengers and where it went.

I also thought about sudden death. Most of us are like this orange
sun outside. We use up our fuel trying to live our lives.
We can burn ourselves up easily. Stars quit and their light
goes out. I am sure that many of the people on that plane
were not prepared for what comes next. I hope they got mercy.
I know that I would not be ready and would need someone to help me.

Wardrobe

The art deco wardrobe was dirty, it couldn't stand up
on its own, abandoned, it was salvage, I cleaned it,
fixed one of its feet, thought about old houses
without closets, perhaps in New York City,
a man putting in his suit, shirts, socks, wallet,
belt, the black shoes, polish, a tie or two, a couple
of photos, a paperback, the pocketknife, a few
dollars, a smoke, maybe a working man,
boots, gloves, blue shirts with the company name
on them, a lunch pail, thermos, rented room,
a hot plate, a hallway, shared restroom, subway
sound outside, a café, listening to police siren
at night, chatter, a blue neon at the local bar.

It was illuminated, a light started to shine when
I wiped the dirt off, stood it up, filled it with
folded towels, sheets, and blankets, put a TV
antenna on top, the big round oval in a
darker brown in the wardrobe at the top where
the tuxedo cat likes to be, looking out the
window over the yellow roses for birds,
people walking their dogs, carrying groceries,
holding their children's hands with big smiles.

Here in the Sun Belt more people are getting sick,
looking for work, trying to not get evicted, live
in their car, it is hot outside, it is summer,
they are angry, it seems like we are all in a
black and white noir, things get out of control,
we are caught up in it, getting hurt, looking for
an escape, just getting by like I think everyone was
doing in this country years ago when the economy
was bad, there was war, suffering, when men,
women wanted help like they want today, some
food, money, a job, a place to stay, a movie to
watch, calm, rest, when we must make hard choices,
forgive, give mercy, when there is desperation,
people die, when we understand how flawed
we really are, in need of some lemon polish,
of hope, of being restored to use like this wardrobe was.

Last Day

On the last day it was raining,

on the last day I was the
last man on earth in
the pandemic, like in the
movie, trying to not
get infected, Vincent Price
running from vampires,
zombies, staying alive,

I felt like the gray fox
that I saw in the city after
buying two slices of
pepperoni pizza, the only
one, hiding, disappearing,

I felt like I will end up
in the hospital, like a
white pig that I saw shot,
scalded, sliced up to eat,

on the last day a few red
leaves in a gray tree,
the milk colored sunshine,
cold, hard for the night
to get down, like medicine,
and later heads exploding,
the blue, red, silver pieces
falling, the fireworks,
illegal, loud, like gunshots,
like the murders on our
street, struggle, it is
our war, our survival, the
police on the way blaring,

on the last day of the year
when the calendar opens
big, better into a pink
flower, our hope, our
optimism, the white tree
outside with orange leaves on it.

Something Simple

The days are getting longer and longer,

a deputy marshal got a shave after
killing a man on the Western.

I want something simple like when
my grandfather sliced open a
watermelon with a big knife on
his front porch one summer day,

special like a silver dollar used to be
or a can of peaches for a
cowboy on the trail and sleeping out.

On the news people are looking for
justice and are fighting the police,

the police are throwing tear gas and
are trying to keep us safe
from rioters and the looters.

My father told me once that a German
prisoner stole one of his father's
watermelons in Texas during WWII,

he thought he needed it.

I want something simple like a slice
of cantaloupe or to go to a used
bookstore with an orange cat
sleeping on the counter,

something good and peaceful,

on the gardening show they are
looking at a Cherokee Chief
red flowering dogwood
and then a batch of yellow flag irises.

A Hot Day

On the buckled sidewalks,
between the breaks, is
orange paint. The small
red roses are still bright
and I am inside with the
air conditioner. On the
wall they are picking
tea leaves, gathering
white flowers, a man
wearing a yellow straw
hat is planting seed
from a cloth bag, a
woman has red peppers
spread out on a
towel on the ground,
a cowboy is returning
to his house and a slow
turning windmill on a tired
horse, and a man is
rowing a boat in indigo
blue on the water close
to the palm trees. I am
reading Elizabeth Bowen's
book *The Heat of the Day*.
I will soon monitor a test
on the computer in the
pandemic. Underneath me
they are lifting the
foundation with jacks,
working on the plumbing,
telling us not to flush
the toilets. Outside it is
still bent, burning,
swelling and pain until this is over.

Orange Flame

Air,

ash

from
the black and burnt
bodies,

and then years later at the Alamo we see
orange and white koi,

ice cream,
peaches,

in the water looking up
at us,

mouths moving,

as if telling us that they
were given
a choice,

and that fish are not as
scary as

dead men.

Stray

String of the big bulb lights,

stretched out in the lonely
night on the empty street,

strung along the roof of
the little wooden house in
a desolate time, strange
stray stars are causing fear,

alone in my truck, I can
see a raccoon cross ahead
of me, then in a yard, a
little rain is coming down,

I almost expect to see a
wagon, horses, coming to
pick up the dead bodies
in the time of the pandemic,

structure, stress, people
are suffering, losing jobs,
the evictions, the freeway
and turn, they are sleeping
up and down the big
road, a different kind of
Christmas lights, in tents,
on the ground, all cold,

I am a solitary man on
my way home, looking at
lights, wondering which
bulb will go out next,
burn out, orange, yellow,
blue, red, which one of us.

City Sky

It is the cold
clumped
mashed potatoes in the sky,

warmed up by the microwave with
all the strange
things up there,

some butter and the gods
eat up most of the potatoes and the chicken
fried steak with the white gravy from
the TV dinner on the blue plate,

the thin sun above is like
something after social upheaval,
cooked up in a corporation's lab,
or an explosion with
some of the yellow light
remaining with the
toxic chemicals frenzied in it,

then my headache lifts just a little
with fewer clouds to
obscure my thinking
which is usually caused
by my allergies,

and then tomorrow I will be talking
about the white sheets
drying on the line
with the sun in them
instead of feeling like
they poured white
concrete in me,

my head like white
flowers
opening up
in the air that
I wish was cleaner.

The Gas Station

The city,

the heat,
the traffic,
the gasoline fumes,

the condom machine,
the telephone numbers on the wall,
the dirty, black towel,

the cigarettes and the smell,
the barbed wire,
the men spitting tobacco juice on the ground,

it was a little boy with a bottle of grape soda getting
back into the green truck with the cold air conditioner,
a Hank Williams song on the radio,
all four of us squeezed together like pickles in a jar,
and then there was the pretty mare, her colt, brown,
white feet, white star, eating grass next to the big women's prison.

Agaves

The big agaves
died in
the snow,

they have
a touch of blue
in them like
I see in my
face and
sky on a cold day,

in my blue jeans,

in the faces of
those that
leave us,

it would be nice if one of them
had this cowbell
that my grandfather
put on one of the white
cows to find them
in the pines,

that we could hear them,

this little boy that
died from abuse
in an apartment
near me last week,

that he,

the agaves
could come back,

that this bougainvillea that
belonged to
my mother
would bloom
pink again this spring.

Candle

In this long life we live,

in the next one a
nice person will
burn like this
flame in a
white candle,

in a dark world,

in a house of ice
without power it is
a yellow light in a
white skull on the
table made in a high
school woodshop
class and sitting
on a pane of glass,

in Posada's drawings,

in the white wax with
the blue flowers
on it when it is
10 degrees outside
with snow on the
ground in blue
light when we
know someone
will die in the
night cold and go on,

in this other place
sharing their light
like this small Day
of the Dead candle
that I bought in
the grocery store
because I thought
it was pretty and it
did not cost much money.

Spin

I want to go on forever,
spin as if a bucking
horse, a Coke bottle,
a piñata, yellow and
full of candy in a tree,
in a motor, to be part
of something that is
big, special, as if a
Neptune, to spin out
of this galaxy, on a
blue record player,
to never end, to spin
like a basketball, on a
windmill in Texas,
slow, bringing up the
water for the thirsty
cows, to do good, to
be happy, that there
is a plan for me,
not feel like a used up
fan belt, tire, in an
old truck that is giving
out, spin, spin like
on a spinning wheel,
in a wagon, adobe
walls, on a ranch,
a blanket for the baby,
some desolate place,
I want to spin
like when I was a
little boy, as if a
wooden top, green
red, until I was dizzy,
and didn't know yet
how hard things can get.

Gives

As if
abandoned
and alone,

the bulb burns
hanging on a black wire
and swinging
from a high ceiling,

with flying cockroaches
on yellowish walls in a cold kitchen
when it is turned off,

and the only light is in a white refrigerator,

the moon outside,

I think a light bulb is like a man's life
when he gives out
and the depleted bulb
is replaced
with a new one,

what a difference
he makes,

why people need her,

enough light to fry some eggs
on a gas stove
with a blue flame
or to get out of bed for
a glass of water
with flowers on it,

how hard it is,

a woman dies
and another
one is born to give.

Today

The surprise visit of the hummingbird
to the red hibiscus on my porch in a
year of three murders on this street
and the stress of the pandemic is
as special to me as when I opened
a package of baseball cards for the
first time with the stick of gum that
I knew would give me a sugar rush.

If you stretch some it is like me looking
at the Matisse painting of the woman
in the red shirt at the art museum in
San Antonio with my family before
we went on and I ate three cheese
enchiladas in the Mexican restaurant.

I forgot to tell you that a few months
before that my daughter sent me a
postcard from Costa Rica with a
hummingbird and a red flower on it
and she talked about how she rode a
horse with the name of Estrellita.

She also told me that someone stole
two red peppers and some cucumbers
today from her plot in the community
garden and I thought about this old
red tractor that my father used to
have that he was always working on.

It was the yellow flowers that the
hummingbird came for last summer
and I guess it would be best if
I didn't know that I was helping
someone when I get a chance like
this in the next life and here is the
cat with her red tongue jumping
up on my desk to assist with this poem.

The Long Drive

The burning orange sun in the morning,
white cloud like a shark on the
bottom of the black sky threatening,
a gunmetal color that made me think
of lawmen and outlaws, what I
saw on the long drive to go to
work, and the transformer blowing
up white sparks, eating fast food,
a man in the backhoe digging a grave
in the cemetery in the night with
the yellow lights by the turnoff,
coyotes, a bobcat, the black cows
in the black shade on a hot day,
news, hard rock music, the horses
on the fence post watching me
drive by, flat tires, gas stations,

on the weekends my daughter made
the drive with me, we talked,
I tried to give advice, a little sad
about the situation, hoping that
she knew that I tried to do my best,

the white egret eating fish in the
pond with the tall pines bordering,
the bridge where I hit the deer
next to the little Baptist church,
the riding lawn mower on fire
and the man watching it in his
front yard, road work, delays,
the red cow dead on the side of the
blacktop after getting hit by a car,
and the truck stopped waiting for
the train to pass by with graffiti
on the freight cars by the feed store
with the windows rolled down,

I had to move in with my parents
after the divorce and it was leaving
in the dark and returning in the
dark, long days and long nights,

the barn owl in the oak tree above
me early in the morning, all the stars,
the wild hogs, the bluebonnets,
Indian paintbrushes, buttercups,
boys playing baseball at the field,
the bloodshot eyes, the red moon,
blue heron, the sun going down,
and the orange fox that I saw near
the house, the hard dirt road,
a good Merle Haggard song to listen to.

A Shooting

I put a small piece of peppermint
in the pot with the agave
to drive away mosquitoes,
seemed to work, next to
where I found a frog that
was missing its head, then
the candy disappeared
and the red hibiscus opened,

yesterday the blue and
yellow helicopter circled
around for an hour, the
police looking for a shooter,
later a stabbing on a Sunday,
my faith, hope the same,
listened to Black Sabbath,

they used to put on their
best hats to go to church,
but this isn't a Western town
anymore, I watched
Scooby-Doo instead of the
black and white noir movie,

the Cornell Woolrich paperback
came in the mail, the kind
that was up front in the
library on those thin racks
that turned, the grocery store,
close to the Red Man,
peanuts, and the lemon drops,

they were still looking for
the shooter in the news,
is there any better smell than
new boots, I won't be able
to afford the rent around here
too much longer, all of us
wired, the computer, and
not to each other, ate an ice cream.

ACKNOWLEDGMENTS

1. "The Yellow Bells" — *Thin Air* / *Voices de la Luna*
2. "The Cotton Pickers" — *Red River Review*
3. "At The Church School" — *Pembroke Magazine*
4. "Fear" — *Illuminations*
5. "Duty" — *Kestrel*
6. "The Motor" — *Illuminations*
7. "The Mobile Clinic" — *VOLT*
8. "The Squeeze" — *San Antonio Express-News* / *Houston Chronicle*
9. "A Winter Day" — *Red River Review*
10. "Panther" — *Bacopa Literary Review*
11. "The Wig" — *RHINO*
12. "At The Barbecue Place" — *Illya's Honey*
13. "Sun" — *The Texas Observer*
14. "Glue Sniffers" — *Carcinogenic Poetry*
15. "Warm" — *Tule Review*
16. "Murder At The Old House" — *Pilgrimage*
17. "Fossil" — *The Aurorean*
18. "Rationing Electricity in Honduras" — *Flare: The Flagler Review*
19. "Undiminished" — *Huizache*
20. "Scratch Off" — *Slow Trains Literary Journal*
21. "Milk Dish" — *Pilgrimage*
22. "The Afterlife" — *The Christian Science Monitor*
23. "Android" — *PANK*
24. "The Transfer" — *Literary Juice*
25. "The Politics of Scarcity" — *Red River Review*
26. "Dutch Oven" — *Slow Trains Literary Journal*
27. "Visit to Rome" — *Nerve Cowboy*
28. "As If In Solitary Confinement" — *The Chaffin Journal*
29. "Blue In The Night" — *Sin Fronteras/Writers Without Borders*
30. "Snap" — *Illya's Honey*
31. "An Honor" — *Rio Grande Review*
32. "Yellow Jackets" — *Blueline*
33. "Fourth Grade" — *The Chaffin Journal*
34. "Navigation" — *Southern Poetry Review*
35. "Silence" — *Dark Matter*
36. "City Lights" — *Carcinogenic Poetry*

37.	"Down There"	*Voices de la Luna*
38.	"Fight For The Water Hole"	*The Chaffin Journal*
39.	"Easter Island"	*The Offbeat*
40.	"Social Worker"	*Star 82 Review*
41.	"The Western"	*The Cape Rock*
42.	"The Old Men"	*Red River Review*
43.	"Splendor"	*The Shangri-La Shack Literary Arts Journal*
44.	"Butterscotch Sun"	*Illya's Honey*
45.	"Baritone"	*The Ocotillo Review*
46.	"Door"	*Visions International California Quarterly*
47.	"Begonia"	*Main Street Rag*
48.	"Testers"	
49.	"Library"	
50.	"A Big Thing"	
51.	"Drift"	
52.	"Coyote"	*Sin Fronteras/Writers Without Borders*
53.	"Purple Lights"	*Cenizo Journal*
54.	"A Cross"	
55.	"Alien Denies Predestination"	*Oyez Review*
56.	"Blue Light Dancer"	
57.	"Coffee Can"	*Cenizo Journal*
58.	"When It Doesn't Rain"	*Cenizo Journal*
59.	"Blue"	*Tejascovido*
60.	"Light and Dark"	
61.	"Indian Blanket"	*Cenizo Journal*
62.	"Old Pictures"	*Louisiana Literature*
63.	"Coneflower"	*El Portal Literary Journal*
64.	"Ice Cream"	*Cenizo Journal*
65.	"Bus Driver"	*Green Hills Literary Lantern*
66.	"Glue"	*Green Hills Literary Lantern*
67.	"Afternoon Shower"	*Streetlight Magazine*
68.	"Light Depressed"	*Eclectica Magazine*
69.	"Pie"	*West Trade Review*
70.	"Bomb"	
71.	"Wardrobe"	*Delta Poetry Review*
72.	"Last Day"	
73.	"Something Simple"	*The Dead Mule School of Southern Literature*

74.	"A Hot Day"	
75.	"Orange Flame"	
76.	"Stray"	
77.	"City Sky"	*Main Street Rag*
78.	"The Gas Station"	
79.	"Agaves"	*2River*
80.	"Candle"	*2River*
81.	"Spin"	
82.	"Gives"	*Concho River Review*
83.	"Today"	*Main Street Rag*
84.	"The Long Drive"	*Hamilton Stone Review*
85.	"A Shooting"	

Benjamin Nash started writing poetry at about the age of 40 years old. This is his first published book of poetry. He is a member of the Austin Poetry Society and enjoys growing flowers. His poems have appeared in *Louisiana Literature, Concho River Review, Pembroke Magazine, Kestrel, Illuminations, VOLT, RHINO, 2River, Blueline, Visions International, The Texas Observer, Streetlight Magazine, Green Hills Literary Lantern, Southern Poetry Review, Voices de la Luna, The Cape Rock, Tule Review, Hamilton Stone Review,* and various other literary journals. Most of his poems are about everyday life experiences.

Benjamin Nash first became interested in poetry in a class at the University of Houston. It was years later that he started to write. At some point he decided that he wanted to share his poetry. This book is his opportunity. Most of these poems are about his life in Texas, the blend of rural and city life, and the struggles we all face.

www.ingramcontent.com/pod-product-compliance
Lightning Source LLC
Chambersburg PA
CBHW020858160426
43192CB00007B/974